LATIMER STUDIES 65

THE NEW TE ___ α
SLAVERY:

APPROACHES AND
IMPLICATIONS

> Mankind is so fallen that no man can be trusted with unchecked power over his fellows. Aristotle said that some people were only fit to be slaves. I do not contradict him. But I reject slavery because I see no men fit to be masters.
>
> *C. S. Lewis, Present Concerns*

BY MARK MEYNELL

The Latimer Trust

© Mark Meynell 2007

ISBN 9780946307593

Published by the Latimer Trust

PO Box 26685

London N14 4XQ

www.latimertrust.org

CONTENTS

Acknowledgements

This project has been in existence for ten years, originally starting out as a Masters Thesis and has since undergone various revisions and applications. The original supervisor was Antony Billington (Lecturer in Hermeneutics at London School of Theology) whose support and wisdom were invaluable. Since then, various friends and colleagues have offered helpful advice and suggestions. I am very grateful to: Hugh Palmer, Paul Blackham, Melinda Hendry, Andrew Burkinshaw, Paul Carter, Adam Johnson and last but certainly not least, my wife Rachel. Finally, I am very grateful to the team at Langham Partnership for their fellowship and support and to the Latimer Trust for the opportunity to revisit this important subject.

I. Introduction: The Slavery Controversy

'Clear biblical teaching' and 'biblical morality' are not
phrases of recent origin. They have been used in the
debates over the centuries on a wide variety of issues
... The clear teaching of the Bible also *had to be
overcome* before slavery and segregation could be
ended and before women could escape their second-
class status. In a remarkably similar pattern today, a
major impediment to the quest for justice and the full
acceptance for gay and lesbian people in the life of
this society is the Bible, which is quoted over and over
again to justify the homophobic prejudice that still so
deeply infects our culture. *Bishop John Selby Spong*[1]

The 200th anniversary of the Abolition of the Slave Trade Bill
arrived amidst great fanfare and rejoicing – and rightly so. The
achievements of the Christian abolitionists like Thomas
Clarkson, William Wilberforce and Olaudah Equiano (to name
but three) certainly deserve recognition. There are, sadly, few
other social breakthroughs with which Christians can be so
closely identified. While many modern historians struggle to
understand or acknowledge their religious fervour (for, as one
spin-doctor said on behalf of his Prime Minister, 'We don't do
God'), there can be little doubt that this was what drove the
activism of many of the abolitionists.[2] Christians can be justly

---

[1] "Scripture is not the ally Christian homophobes think it is", John Selby
Spong (http://www.baptistwatch.org/content/biblegay.html) – my italics.
[2] See, for instance, John Coffey's excellent introduction to the issue: "The
abolition of the slave trade: Christian conscience and political action."
Cambridge Papers 15:2 (June 2006)

proud of what was achieved.

However, slavery as an institution also stands as a blight on Christian history. Worse still, it is appears to stand as a blight on the Bible itself. The Bible appears to endorse, and perhaps even advocate, slavery. This was certainly the contention of many devoutly Christian, *slave-owning* Confederates fighting in the American Civil War. Of course, the evangelical abolitionists were equally insistent that the Bible sustained their own position. The problem was that two mutually exclusive positions were derived from the same book! The implications of this are significant, the questions unsettling. What are we to make of the Bible's stance(?s) on slavery? Is the Bible invalidated by its teaching on the issue? Is it even possible to articulate a 'biblical morality' so dismissingly alluded to by Bishop Spong? Unsurprisingly, many modern evangelicals have lost their confidence in Scripture over of this issue.

Of course, it would be hard to find many serious biblical advocates today of a position akin to that of the slave-owners in America's Deep South. The institution of slavery is now regarded as actually *sinful*. However, while this is a long-past ethical debate, it has a crucial relevance for various contemporary debates in Christian ethics. This is most usefully illustrated by the Australian theologian Kevin Giles,[3] who makes a convincing case for moving away from the traditional view of the role of women,[4] on the basis of parallels with the slavery

---

[3] He has written extensively on the subject, for instance, *The Trinity & Subordinationism* (Downers Grove, IVP, 2002). For the purposes of this booklet, I will confine myself to his article "The Biblical argument for Slavery" in *Evangelical Quarterly* Vol 66:1 (1994).
[4] As expounded, for example, in Piper & Grudem, *Recovering Biblical Manhood and Womanhood*, (Wheaton, Crossway, 1991) pp 31-59.

debate. Again, we find two sides, drawing very different conclusions from one book. Giles wonders, quite understandably, whether or not Christians 100 years hence will look back on the contemporary debates about the role of women with similar disbelief.

While the question of the role of women still divides many within the church, it is now the issue of homosexuality that is more pressing and pastorally even more fraught. Intriguingly, what is essentially the same slavery argument is often put forward. Bishop Spong, for one, does so frequently[5] as do many involved in defending the current Bishop of New Hampshire, Gene Robinson. Their basis is commonly the 'trajectory' model, whereby the biblical writers are discerned to be advocating change, perhaps only one step at a time.[6] The interpreter's task is to trace the trajectory beyond the pages of the closed canon of Scripture. Hence, if liberation from oppression is deemed to be the agenda, the liberation of slaves can be followed up with the liberation of women and after that, victims of homophobia. This is certainly what provoked William Webb's recent publication, *Slaves, Women & Homosexuals*.[7] The ethical issues surrounding each of the three groups of people are clearly connected. But to what extent?

---

[5] See J.S. Spong, *Rescuing the Bible from Fundamentalism* (San Francisco, Harper, 1991) p 101.

[6] See France's use of the *trajectory* approach in his discussion of Acts 15 (R.T. France, *Women in the Church's Ministry* (Carlisle, Paternoster, 1995) pp 17-18, 92). This approach has parallels with Tom Wright's model of performance and improvisation of a new five act Shakespeare play (N.T. Wright, *The New Testament & The People of God* (London, SPCK, 1993) pp 140-141).

[7] William J. Webb, *Slaves, Women & Homosexuals – Exploring the Hermeneutics of Cultural Analysis* (Downers Grove, IVP 2001).

Since it is impossible to address all the challenges and questions raised by the slavery debate in a single Latimer booklet, my aim is limited. I seek specifically to evaluate the legitimacy of using the slavery argument to counter traditional ethical positions. Because Giles' focus is slavery's relationship to the role of women and not homosexuality *per se*, that issue will form the centre of gravity for this booklet. If there is a direct link, the trajectory model might possibly stand. If not, the trajectory of liberation has broken down here, and therefore the abolition of slavery is not the grounds on which to reject a traditional position on homosexuality.

2. Slavery: Ancient Rome and the American Deep South Compared

2.1. Connotations and Cultural Baggage

The word 'race' provokes many reactions today, often because of issues of injustice, discrimination and inequality.[8] This is sadly true even at the start of the twenty-first century. It is not so long ago that there existed a regime whose whole legislative and political system was intrinsically discriminatory – South Africa. Furthermore, as recently as May 1997, President Clinton accepted corporate responsibility for a 1930s *government* programme to use syphilis-suffering African-Americans in the Alabama town of Tuskegee as laboratory animals (a programme known as the Tuskegee Syphilis Study). The experiment has had huge implications for race tensions in

---

[8] This was highlighted through the findings of the Inquiry into the racially motivated murder of Stephen Lawrence in 1993, and the public reaction to the 2005 killing of Anthony Walker in Liverpool.

that area.

Yet, the word's original sense was far less inflammatory, often merely used as a means of distinguishing between people groups in the fledgling science of anthropology. Emotional heat became attached to issues of race. This is not surprising – connotations and semantic ranges of words invariably change over time. The same has happened with the very idea of slavery.

2.2. The Problem of Slavery

When the Bible, and Paul in particular, makes statements about slaves, the temperature of contemporary readers inevitably rises. At best, it seems distant and alien, at worst, morally repugnant and offensive. Consequently, Paul's provocative use of the metaphor of slavery for a Christian's relationship to God seems simply inexplicable.[9] For example, Keith Bradley, in his work on ancient Roman slavery, writes:

> The unwillingness of Christians to tamper with slavery ... is apparent most starkly of all in their adoption of slavery imagery to describe and symbolise their relationship with their God.[10]

Why was Paul tolerant of such a situation?[11]

The question often rouses moral indignation against

---

[9] E.g. Philippians 1:1; cf. F. Lyall, *Slaves, Citizens and Sons* (Grand Rapids, Zondervan, 1984) p 27ff.

[10] K. Bradley, *Slavery & Society at Rome* (Cambridge, CUP, 1994) p 152.

[11] For a recent study of Paul's use of the slavery metaphor, see Murray J Harris' excellent contribution to IVP's *New Studies in Biblical Theology*. "Slave of Christ – a New Testament metaphor for total devotion to Christ" (Leicester, Apollos, 1999).

Paul amongst contemporary writers because he has been used to endorse morally dubious and indefensible practices in recent centuries, such as in the Deep South of the United States. It is very easy to read the apostle as spinelessly upholding slavery's status quo, and then to hoist him on the petard of his convictions about the equality of all humanity, whether 'slave or free'.[12] There were critics of the institution of slavery even in Paul's time, as many modern scholars are quick to point out.[13] Roman Stoic philosophers were notable for their concern for slaves' conditions. The most famous was Seneca the Younger, a Roman Senator and scholar in the early Republic who was subsequently forced to commit suicide by the Emperor Nero. If a pagan philosopher at the heart of the Roman Empire could be vocal about the plight of slaves, could not a Christian apostle follow suit, especially one professing higher ideals about personhood?

2.3.   Similar Institutions?

Let us begin by asking whether slavery in every century can be understood in similar terms. What characterised slavery at the time of Paul? Could this help us to understand Paul's rather unsettling attitude to slavery?

Many have undertaken such a comparison, though with a wide variety of motives. Some scholars even use one slave culture to understand another, confident in the parallels. Bradley, for one, explicitly sets out to do this. As a classical

---

[12] Galatians 3:28.

[13] E.g. Crouch, *The Origin and Intention of the Colossian Haustafel,* Vandenhoeck & Ruprecht, 1972); Westermann, *The Slave Systems of Greek & Roman Antiquity* (American Philosophical Society, 1955); Parsons, "Slavery and the New Testament", *Vox Evangelica* (1988).

scholar seeking insights into the life of the Roman slave, he draws on the experiences of African American slaves, assuming (however dubiously) their similarities.[14]

However, it is not just classical scholars who do this. Swartley collated the writings of various people on both sides of the slavery debate in the last few centuries showing that the link was made by both factions. From the pro-slavery side, one Governor Hammond from South Carolina. Hammond sees clear continuity between the Bible's culture of slavery (which, of course, ranged from the world of the Old Testament patriarchs to the early Roman Empire) and the slavery he advocated in his own day:

> It is impossible ... to suppose that Slavery is contrary to the will of God. It is equally absurd to say that American Slavery differs in form or principle from that of the chosen people. We accept the Bible terms as the definition of our Slavery, and its precepts as the guide of our conduct.[15]

To defend what he regards as self-evident, he insists that there has never been the slightest change in the 3000-year old culture of slavery.

Speaking for the opposition stands one George Bourne, a Presbyterian minister from Virginia.

> Finally, we say that slavery is never an act of benevolence. The testimony of a thousand witnesses presented in *American Slavery As It Is* shows that slavery is one of the basest, most oppressive, cruel, and inhumane institutions known to humanity. As Bourne says, "slavery, however

---

[14] Bradley, *Slavery & Society at Rome* pp 7-8.
[15] W.M. Swartley, *Slavery, Sabbath, War & Women* (Pennsylvania, Herald Press, 1983) p 35; quoting from Hammond's Letters in *The Pro-Slavery Argument* (1852, repub. New York, Negro Universities Press, 1968)

supported by use of 'isolated passages' is against the spirit of the Scriptures".[16]

Working in the opposite direction, Bourne transposes the worst excesses of Deep South slavery to every instance of slavery in world history. Slavery then becomes *necessarily* "oppressive, cruel, and inhumane."

2.4. The Similarities Examined

What similarities were there between the slave economies of Ancient Rome and the American Deep South?

(i) Origins

There are certainly parallels in the origins of slavery in both societies. The need for labour increased as both empires grew, and so slaves were drawn from whatever sources were at hand. So, the late Roman Empire drew in slaves from all over the peripheries of the burgeoning Empire in order to sustain such widespread growth.[17] A Roman slave was far more likely to find himself or herself in such a predicament as the result of conquest or raids than because of punishment or self-sale.[18] Similarly, Great Britain required increasing numbers of slaves to provide labour in her colonies and consequently drew on the only market available – West Africa.

---

[16] Swartley, *Slavery, Sabbath, War & Women* p 46, quoting Bourne's *Condensed Anti-Slavery Argument,* (New York, S. W. Benedict, 1845) pp 54-55

[17] Lyall, *Slaves, Citizens and Sons* p 28; T. Sowell, *Race and Culture: A World View* (Basic Books, New York, 1994) p 217.

[18] Sowell, *Race and Culture: A World View* p 193.

(ii)   *Forfeited Autonomy*

The most obvious similarity lies in the control that masters had over their slaves. The nature of slavery is such that the enslaved individual has lost all personal autonomy by definition. It is this characteristic which causes most indignation today. In Rome, the indignity of the slave's status was enshrined in law, and was greatly influenced by ideas of the slave propagated by Aristotle, who regarded them as 'living tools'.[19] So for instance, the Roman lawyer Gaius, writing near the time of the apostle Paul, taught that:

> the most basic distinction in law of persons is that all men are either slaves or free ... Slaves are in the *potestas* [or power] of their masters.[20]

Such power was originally regarded as absolute.[21] Roman law held that a slave-owner had rights to put a disobedient slave to death, the grounds for which were entirely at the owner's discretion.[22] It is no wonder, then, that Paul saw the 'yoke of slavery' (1 Timothy 6:1) as something to be avoided: 'You were bought at a price; do not become slaves of men'.[23] (1

---

[19] P.T. O'Brien, *Colossians & Philemon* WBC (Dallas, Word, 1982) p 193.
[20] Gaius *Institutes* 1.9, 1.52ff – this book forms the most complete legal work from that era.
[21] Although it is to be remembered that as the Empire progressed, there were at least one or two instances of owners being taken to court for *unjustly* putting their slaves to death. This trend seems to have started under Augustus. However, this was rare, and never undermined the general principles laid down.
[22] N.T. Wright, *Colossians & Philemon* TNTC (Leicester, IVP, 1986) p 166.
[23] As will be shown, there were several material advantages to slavery which may well have appealed to a persecuted Christian, for example. This helps to explain why Paul sees the need to warn the Corinthians against succumbing to the temptation voluntarily to enter servitude.

Corinthians 7:23)

An American slave-owner wielded similar power. The effects on the enslaved were profound, both personally and culturally. Being forced to acquire the European names of their owners was just the start. Life was brutal and above all unpredictable and resale always a possibility. The fluctuating fortunes or discretion of masters meant that the threat of families being broken up was real. Slaves would often be forced to find partners outside their own plantation, as the most common unit of slaves in any one place was less than 20. This might mean that the father would visit his family only once a week. It was hard enough to be divorced from their wider kinship ties (which are still so important to African culture), but for husbands and wives, or parents and children to be indefinitely separated, was a bitter pill.

(iii)   *The Extent of Slave Ownership*

Bradley boldly states that there have only ever been five slave societies in world history, in the technical sense – namely Classical Athens, Classical Italy, The Caribbean, Brazil and the United States.[24] He estimates the proportion of slaves with a minimum adult slave population of 20% constituting a 'slave society'. It is significant that Bradley highlights Classical Italy, but not the rest of the Roman Empire – indeed slavery was not as prevalent in the ancient Mediterranean as one might expect. Likewise, as Parish's statistics show, in nineteenth century America, 'half of the total number of slaveholders owned no more than five slaves each.'[25] Three quarters of white

---

[24] Bradley, *Slavery & Society at Rome* p 12
[25] Parish, *Slavery – the many faces of a southern institution* (Dundee, British

southerners owned no slaves at all[26], and perhaps most surprising of all, there were a quarter of a million free African Americans living and working in the Deep South.[27]

These statistics are cited not to minimise slavery's significance. For with such high proportions of slaves in the two societies, it would be impossible for the culture of slavery not to have had an impact on those who lived alongside it. Their use is merely to restrain wild imaginations.

2.5. Vital Contrasts

After this brief survey, it is not hard to see why some are quick to assume other parallels between Rome and the Deep South, despite the lack of corroborative evidence. Basing substantial conclusions on the rough equivalence of the two societies is not only speculative, but on closer inspection, it is also flawed.

(i) Calls for Abolition

Ancient Rome never witnessed an abolition movement. The moral crusade of the last two centuries is unique in world history, the abolition of slavery an unprecedented achievement. Although Seneca argued that slaves were *essentially* free human beings, and therefore that cruel slave-owners were exceeding the bounds of moral rectitude, he and his fellow Stoics *never* questioned slavery itself. They merely sought to curb its excesses in classic stoic fashion. We must understand Paul within this context. There was no opposition to the

---

Association for American Studies, 1979) p 7
[26] Parish, *Slavery – the many faces of a southern institution* p 13
[27] Parish, *Slavery – the many faces of a southern institution* p 7

principle of slavery in his society, and nor had there been before him. 'Hardly anyone considered the system optional or thought of an alternative.'[28]

(ii)   Social Flexibility or An Inescapable Trap?

Because of contemporary images of slavery, one of the hardest aspects of ancient slavery to grasp is its flexibility and social ambiguity. For instance, apart from the Senatorial or *Eques* (knights) classes,[29] there would be no visible means of distinguishing between slaves and freemen;[30] it would only perhaps be possible to identify their profession. Furthermore, no specific vocations were either exclusive or barred to slaves[31] (with the one exception of military service[32]). It was therefore not uncommon to find slaves in highly skilled professions. For instance, the red-glaze pottery workshops of Arretium gained their fame because of the highly gifted slaves who worked in them. Potters would inscribe their names on their work, and many had Eastern names, probably Greek slaves brought over specifically for their skills.[33]

Yet, while most slaves were manual labourers, the

---

[28] A. Lincoln, *Ephesians* WBC (Dallas, Word, 1990), p 415.

[29] They wore togas with purple stripes.

[30] Lyall, *Slaves, Citizens and Sons* p 35.

[31] D. Martin, *Slavery as Salvation* (New Haven, Yale University Press, 1990) p 11.

[32] Bradley, *Slavery & Society at Rome* p 65. This was intriguingly in contrast to other slave societies, which were prepared to rely on slaves to command their armies – e.g. the Ottoman Empire – Sowell, *Race and Culture: A World View* p 190.

[33] Bradley, *Slavery & Society at Rome* p 64; cf. Westermann, *The Slave Systems of Greek & Roman Antiquity* p 120.

institution did not restrict them to such work. As the Empire developed, it was not uncommon for slaves to attain astonishing power, despite being legally bound to their masters' *potestas*.[34] Along with political power and influence came great wealth, and some even possessed a household of slaves of their own.[35] Consequently, scholars now refer to the 'upwardly mobile slave', not least because of his (they were predominantly male) frequent appearance in ancient literature as objects of ridicule. It is telling that Petronius' *Satyricon* takes such delight in his protagonist, Trimalchio, a wealthy freedman glorying in his enslaved past, because the original readers would all have recognized the character. Furthermore, modern scholarship has unearthed many historical examples of slaves climbing the social pyramid. Thus, Felix, the procurator of Judea, with whom Paul has dealings in Acts 23-24, had been a freedman of Claudius.[36]

Yet this phenomenon was unthinkable in the pre-Civil War American Deep South, for at least two reasons. Firstly, there is a marked contrast between Roman and American attitudes to the slave-free divide. For talented Roman slaves, the prospect of freedom was very real, and manumissions were far more common in Rome than in the States. Secondly, the Roman patronage system meant that *everyone* (whether slave or free) had obligations to someone higher up in the social pecking order, all the way up to the Emperor. Thus, in his highly influential thesis, Bartchy makes the following remarks about first century Corinth:

---

[34] D. Stanley S.J., "Imitation in Paul's Letters" in Richardson & Hurd (ed), *From Jesus to Paul* (Ontario, Laurier University Press, 1984) p 131.
[35] Martin, *Slavery as Salvation* p 10.
[36] Lyall, *Slaves, Citizens and Sons* p 27.

"Were you a slave when you were called?" Among the ideas which have distorted both the modern comprehension of slavery in the Greek and Roman world and the meaning of 1 Corinthians 7:21, are the assumptions that there was a wide separation between slave and freed-man status, that slaves in general were badly treated, and that everyone enslaved was trying to free himself from his bondage. None of these assumptions are true for first century Corinth.[37]

Compare these observations with those of the *Dictionary of Afro-American Slavery*, itself contrasting the plight of African slaves in the States, and the inter-tribal slaves in West Africa:

> The status [back in Africa] of slave, adopted outsider, and full tribal member merged into one another, and the specific rights a slave might have (to start a family, join a kin group, bear free children) varied from place to place. West Africans, then, had little experience with the *absolute dichotomy* of free persons and slaves they would discover as chattels in North America.[38]

(iii) Racism

Fundamental to this 'absolute dichotomy' was of course race. In Rome, a slave's race was hardly ever at issue. As Sowell noted, 'slavery flourished in ancient Greece and Rome without any racial ideology.'[39] An Italian might own another Italian, or a Briton, or an African. Furthermore, there was no intrinsic reason why a wealthy African would not own an Italian slave.

---

[37] S.S. Bartchy,   – *1st Century and the Interpretation of 1 Corinthians 7:21* (Missoula, Society of Biblical Literature, 1973) pp 114-115.
[38] A. Kulikoff, "Slave Family" in *Dictionary of Afro-American Slavery* (ed. R.M. Miller and J.D.Smith, New York, Greenwood, 1980) p 228 – my highlighting.
[39] Sowell, *Race and Culture: A World View* p 194.

There was no such parallel in the United States. A free black might own a black slave;[40] a black owning a white was inconceivable. That was axiomatic in American slavery. So, in addition to defending the practice of slavery, the main proponents asserted racial justifications, like the Confederacy's Vice President, Alexander Stephens: 'the Negro is not equal to the white man; slavery – subordination to the superior race is his natural and normal condition.'[41]

This inherent racism which meant that slaves, imported or born captive, did not have the potential for escape that their ancient counterparts enjoyed. The colour of a slave's skin marked him indelibly:

> The line of race and colour drawn between master and slave was so firm that the few exceptions did not threaten it.[42] This line dictated the formal rigidity of the master-slave relationship, the difficulty and the rarity of manumission, and the twilight of existence of the free black community ... Bondage was a life sentence and a hereditary one.[43]

This racism generated a profound sense of dread. The 'nagging

---

[40] Loren Schweninger gives the following unexpected statistics. 'Although only a small percentage of free Negroes ever owned other blacks, and though only a tiny proportion of those who did ever possessed more than a few slaves, by 1830, 3,775 free blacks in the United States (almost all of them in the Southern states) owned approximately 12,760 slaves. At this time the free black population stood at 182,070, probably representing 35,000 or 40,000 families. Thus, about one out of ten free black family heads owned at least one bondsman.' Schweninger, "Black Slaveholders" in *Dictionary of Afro-American Slavery*, p 665.

[41] Giles, "The Biblical argument for Slavery" pp 11-12

[42] Sowell cites the extraordinary case of the black slave who was captain of a Mississippi riverboat with a racially mixed crew in the antebellum south. (Sowell, *Race and Culture: A World View* p 191)

[43] Parish, *Slavery – the many faces of a southern institution* p 11.

fear of servile insurrection',[44] as well as of external interference from the North, dominated many plantation owners (not unlike fear of the *swart-gevaar* ('black threat') felt by the architects of apartheid). This helps to explain the pro-slavers' vigour in the debates as well as the hopelessness of those enslaved. The longer the institution continued, the greater the opposition and therefore the tougher its supporters. Such racist attitudes were by no means unique, of course, and had been inherited from the various Empires which controlled the Atlantic slave trade. But they have become so ingrained, that they fuel many of the tensions felt in that part of the world to this day. Thus, the Tuskegee experiment is merely one of many rallying points for those who have suffered at the hands of racists.

(iv)   *Hypocrisy and Inconsistency*

It was not merely the racism at the heart of American slavery which made it so obnoxious; it was the hypocrisy that lay behind it. The Deep South economies were so dependent upon slavery that the lofty principles behind the American Revolution and the subsequent drafting of the Constitution might as well never have existed. These had been compartmentalised so that, 'the republican liberties of whites could be kept distinct from the emancipation of enslaved blacks'.[45] Hence, Sowell makes the point that, whereas slavery had existed in nearly every previous society in history in some form or other, American slavery was 'peculiar' 'only because human bondage was inconsistent with the principles on which this nation was

---

[44] Parish, *Slavery – the many faces of a southern institution* p 11.
[45] Parish, *Slavery – the many faces of a southern institution* p 10.

founded'.[46]

However, double standards also existed at the most personal level. Following biblical precedent, there was strong emphasis upon the responsibility of husbands and fathers as the head of the family. However, there was one rule for wealthy white slave-owners, and another for those in their possession. As we have seen, a slave's family unit was nothing more than a mother and her children. A man was cast adrift, because market forces demanded unattached slaves.[47] If a father was sold, he might never see his family again; slave marriages were not recognised in law; nor were familial ties. Together with the sexual abuse of the women in their control by such ostensibly upright owners,

> such familial arrangements undermined the strict Victorian morality that characterised white West European cultures in the nineteenth century.[48]

Various travellers through the Deep South documented what they found as they went 'under cover' from plantation to plantation – one example was Frederick Law Olmsted and his *A Journey in the Back Country*. These writers exposed white hypocrisy as well as slavery's misery and their accounts were instrumental in raising public awareness in Britain and the Northern States. Thus that small group of Evangelicals in Clapham was galvanised to change history.

2.6.   Conclusion

It is clear from this brief survey that despite the similarities, the

---

[46] Sowell, *Race and Culture: A World View* p 186.
[47] Kulikoff, "Slave Family" p 230.
[48] Kulikoff, "Slave Family" p 230.

cultures of slavery in Ancient Rome and the American Deep South were very different. American slavery was plagued by deep-rooted racism and hypocrisy, a charge that simply could not be levelled at its first-century equivalent. This is not to condone the institution at any point in history. Yet it does partly explain why there was no great impetus for the apostle Paul to call for the removal of such a vast and culturally deep-rooted system.[49]

This is not to say that Paul was happy with the *status quo*. As will be seen, he *did* make radical demands on slave-masters, which humanised and ultimately undermined slavery. The question then arises: how much of the *status quo* was he concerned to confront and transform? Whether or not it is possible to differentiate between the three sections of the Household Codes in Ephesians and Colossians is crucial to the wider debate. Do Paul's radical intentions for slaves demand similar changes for the role of women (or by extension, sexual ethics)? So we now move from history to the Bible.

3.   Divided Household Codes: An Exegetical Fallacy?

3.1.   Introduction

In the forthright manner characteristic of his whole essay, Kevin Giles makes the following assertion about the attitudes

---

[49] Even when Wilberforce and his colleagues began, they could only conceive of ridding the world of the terrors of the mid-Atlantic slave trade, and not the whole institution itself. That would have been deemed utopian. Of course, when they began to win the argument, they sought to achieve even greater things. Sowell, *Race and Culture: A World View* p 210.

and arguments of the American Christian Pro-Slavers.

> They reasoned that to reject the commands about slavery called into question the authority also of husbands and parents. It was obvious that the apostles held these matters to be of equal force.[50]

Unfortunately, this telling comment is almost concealed by its appearance in a footnote. Nevertheless, it gets to the heart of the issue:

> As we have noted, most modern day supporters of the permanent subordination of women claim the addresses to slaves are somehow different. This claim is exegetically fallacious and was opposed by the pro-slavery theologians. As far as I can see, they were united in seeing these injunctions as of one kind.[51]

The household instructions or codes of Colossians and Ephesians, and indeed of 1 Peter, have therefore become the battlegrounds for this issue, as they all contain injunctions for both husbands and wives, and slaves and their masters. Is Giles valid in this claim? We will confine ourselves to Paul's letters.

3.2. In Defence of Giles

Fundamental to sound exegesis is the concern to understand a text's context, whether that be cultural or literary. To understand the context of the 'Household Codes', three issues concern us here.

---

[50] Giles "The Biblical argument for Slavery" p 10
[51] Giles "The Biblical argument for Slavery" p 10, footnote 33

(i)   The Household Codes – imported exegetical units?

The fact that at least two different biblical writers use the same literary form is itself telling, and various ancient precedents have been identified.[52] While the extent of their influence is hard to articulate, it is perfectly legitimate to regard the codes as well-worn forms appropriated for Christian ends. So, from a contextual point of view, it would indeed appear fallacious to distinguish between various parts of the codes. Clearly, Paul has in mind some sort of relationship between the three groups of people. He treats each pair in exactly the same way, with the subordinate member of the pair preceding the one in authority. Even the language Paul uses to address each pairing has parallels. It would seem strange to some, therefore, to see a distinction between the groups. As Lincoln insists, they form a literary unit.[53] All three relationships were culturally defined, and Paul simply christianised a culturally recognised unit. The exegetical concerns of the American pro-slavers seem entirely fair. Remove one pair, then stop the others being removed, whether on good theological grounds or not?

But the case does not stop there. At the very least, it would appear that Paul's great pronouncements and ideals about the new status of the Christian are in tension, if not outright conflict, with the household codes.

---

[52] E.g. Ephesians 5:22-6:9; Colossians 3:18-4:1; 1 Peter 2:18-3:7. This dissertation gives Paul the benefit of the doubt as author of Colossians and Ephesians, while acknowledging that there is considerable debate over this issue.

[53] Lincoln, *Ephesians* p 352.

(ii)   *Galatians 3:28 and Colossians 3:11 – An Agenda For Change?*

Steve Motyer articulates the problem:

> [Galatians 3:28] sits very awkwardly beside the household codes of Colossians 3:18-4:1, Ephesians 5:22-6:9 and 1 Peter 2:18-3:7, with their insistence that wives should submit to their husbands, and slaves to their masters.[54]

It certainly seems strange that Paul could write both the household codes and this wonderfully liberating statement of Christian equality in Galatians 3:28. It is especially incongruous in current thinking, as Galatians 3:28 has been dubbed 'the feminist *credo* of equality' in at least one work[55], which reflects the sentiments of many. The key issue is to discern precisely what purpose Paul had in writing these visionary words. Were they designed to supersede the pragmatic and concessive household codes or to be held out as an (eschatological?) goal, while in the meantime the codes maintained some sort of order in a difficult worldly environment?[56] To what extent were they to be manifestos for change in church life? For if they were, then it stands to reason

---

[54] S. Motyer, "The relationship between Paul's gospel of 'all one in Christ Jesus' (Galatians 3:28) and the Household Codes" *Vox Evangelica*, Vol 19 (1989) p 33.

[55] R. Allen & B. Allen, *Liberated Traditionalism* (Portland, Multnomah Press, 1985) p 134.

[56] This seems to be the view of Motyer, who understands the Colossian code within the context of Colossians 3:10. '[T]he new man is constantly at war with the old, and experiences his newness only partially in this age.' (Motyer, "The relationship between Paul's gospel of 'all one in Christ Jesus' (Galatians 3:28) and the Household Codes" p 45) It is only at the eschaton that this war will be resolved of course, but the 'new man' should constantly work hard to overcome the old.

that the oppressive structures to women and slaves should be removed as soon as possible. One half of the problem has been achieved, thanks to the efforts of Wilberforce and countless others. The other half should only take a matter of time but is no less urgent for the church.

After all, there is no question that Paul expected attitudes and practice within the Galatian churches to change as a result of his pronouncement (and we can assume that the same was to go for the church in Colosse). At the heart of the Galatian controversy was confusion over how Gentile converts should relate to their Jewish brethren. Paul was adamant that nothing should stand in the way of the unifying work of Christ on the cross. If Jewish believers cut links with Gentiles, then to all intents and purposes 'Christ died for nothing'. (Galatians 2:21) So, Galatians 3:28 was a challenge to alter their understanding radically – a challenge which even Paul's fellow apostles (like Peter) avoided to their cost.[57] Should the other 'liberated' groups in Galatians 3, namely slaves and women, follow suit? For there can be little doubt that Paul deliberately alluded to the three most visible and deep-rooted distinctions in ancient Roman *and* Jewish society – those of gender, social status and ethnicity.[58] Furthermore, there is evidence to suggest that a degree of restlessness was caused in the churches, amongst the slaves in particular, by such liberating statements.[59] So, Galatians 3:28 and Colossians 3:11 were clearly

---

[57] Galatians 2:11-14.

[58] Witherington points out that Paul takes exactly the same societal divisions in his discussion of marriage in 1 Corinthians 7 (B. Witherington III, *Women in the Earliest Churches* (Society for NT Studies Monograph series, Cambridge, CUP, 1988) p 26).

[59] Some would argue that this explains the very existence of the Haustafeln, written to temper Paul's egalitarian sentiments. Crouch covers the various

written to challenge prevalent attitudes. Do Paul's aims remain unfulfilled nearly two thousand years on?

(iii)   *A Process of Reform?*

It is clear that Paul sought to improve the lot of those his society tended to ignore. This was consistent with a man of great ideals, but who sensed that a complete removal of societal oppression was well beyond his scope and influence. Ralph Martin defends Paul for not calling for abolition because, 'the time was not ripe for the solution of such difficult questions.'[60] Yet Paul did not settle for passive resignation. The household codes were in fact highly subversive in themselves.[61] It is no accident that in each pairing, he addresses the so-called weaker partner first.[62] This is especially significant, because they are clearly regarded as being morally responsible persons, in marked contrast to prevailing contemporary attitudes. In fact, it is astounding that Paul addresses slaves at all.[63] Furthermore, with regard to his attitudes to women, Witherington remarks:

> Paul nowhere exhorts the husband to subject the wife or even order her to submit, nor is the wife told to urge her

---

positions: Crouch, *The Origin and Intention of the Colossian Haustafel* pp 126-129.

[60] R.P. Martin, *Colossians: The Church's Lord and the Christian's Liberty* (Exeter, Paternoster Press, 1972) p 132. The Roman authorities were renowned for being ruthless in their quelling of such uprisings – Spartacus suffered the fate of many others who attempted such *coups*.

[61] O'Brien quotes approvingly the Colossians commentary by Dibelius with reference to Colossians 3:22 on slaves: 'The whole section [on slavery] has been formed out of original Christian ideas.' (O'Brien, *Colossians & Philemon* p 226)

[62] Witherington, *Women in the Earliest Churches* p 50.

[63] Lincoln, *Ephesians* p 413.

husband to be her head. Each party is addressed directly.[64]

At an earlier stage in his work, he notes:

> [We do not] find in the NT any statement about the woman's
> inferiority to man.   Instead of talking about authority,
> Ephesians 5 talks about love and headship, and Colossians 3
> about love.[65]

However, Paul's desire for reform can be seen most clearly in
the presence of reciprocal injunctions to the husband, parent
and master.   In Ephesians, every member of the Christian
household was required to take 5:21 to heart, resulting in some
degree of mutual submission and selfless concern. Then, for
instance, husbands are required to love their wives on an
extraordinarily demanding scale, taking the death of Christ as
both model and motivation (Ephesians 5:25-33).   The slave
master is to remember that his eternal lot is *identical* with that
of his slave, facing the same God at judgment (Colossians 3:25-
4:1 – surely a real encouragement to the downtrodden slave).
Thus, Paul reminds masters that they can no longer expect
immunity when they abuse members of their households. In a
culture where slaves were considered barely human, this was
groundbreaking.

It is not hard to see, therefore, that Paul has a reforming
agenda, despite not setting out to revolutionise his society as
such. Paul was not concerned with slaves' release, but works
for the 'amelioration of their lot.'[66] Many suggest that in order
to be thoroughly faithful to Paul and the biblical record, it is
necessary to complete the process. It is simply a question of
'tracing the trajectory towards equality between men and

---

[64] Witherington, *Women in the Earliest Churches* p 58.
[65] Witherington, *Women in the Earliest Churches* p 46.
[66] O'Brien, *Colossians & Philemon* p 232.

24

women'.[67]

Now is this a responsible handling of these texts? Is there not a real danger of imposing agendas and anachronistic connotations here, just as was noted in the previous chapter? To this we now turn.

3.3. The Case Against Giles

Even within the undisputedly Pauline corpus, the apparent contradictions between the teaching on the roles within the household, and the ideals of the Christian's status before God cannot be ignored. It is indeed curious that the same person could make the symmetrical injunctions to married couples in 1 Corinthians 7, and then in the same letter, write so strongly about the subordination of women in chapters 11 and 14. Was Paul consistent even within this one letter? More importantly, does he have a consistent purpose throughout his letters for the three pairs of relationships dealt with in the household codes? If he does, it should be possible to decide whether or not a division within the codes is permissible. Unless we address these issues, we run the real risk of appealing to selective evidence. As Carson notes:

> As a general rule, the more complex and/or emotional the issue, the greater the tendency to select only part of the evidence, prematurely construct a grid, and so filter the rest of the evidence through the grid that it is robbed of any substance. What is needed is even-handedness, along with a greater desire for fidelity than for originality in the interpretation of the Scriptures.[68]

---

[67] France, *Women in the Church's Ministry* p 92.
[68] D.A. Carson, *Exegetical Fallacies* (Grand Rapids, Baker, 1984) p 98.

(i)   The Attitude to Slavery in the Pauline Corpus

Even within the codes themselves, a degree of gradation can be seen, whereby the three pairings are arranged with the closest relationship coming first (wives/husbands), and the least close coming third (slaves/masters). These concentric circles of relationship hint that, at the very least, some sort of distinction might be possible.

As a former Pharisee, Paul was steeped in an Old Testament worldview, with a particularly intricate knowledge of the Torah. The Old Testament's teaching on slavery stood in marked contrast to other ancient Near Eastern cultures. This will inevitably have influenced Paul's attitudes, as C.J.H. Wright makes clear.[69] A few examples will suffice. The civil laws pertaining to slavery are unparalleled in the ancient world (Exodus 21:20-21, Exodus 21:26-27 and Deuteronomy 23:15-16). The first two take up the cases of slaves assaulted or killed by their own masters. If found guilty, a master was to be punished, which might result in death. That was unheard of at a time when the closest legal equivalents only dealt with assault on *other* people's slaves.[70] The most subversive legal point, however, is found in the Deuteronomy passage. This allowed for a runaway slave to avoid being sent home since the law *commanded* people to provide him with residence elsewhere. This would imply that the institution was not legally sacrosanct or protected. Wright points out that the lot of the Israelite slave was different even from that of his or her Roman or Greek equivalents. Slaves were largely

> residential, domestic workers, complementing, but not a

---

[69] C.J.H. Wright, *Living as the People of God* (Leicester, IVP, 1983) p 182.
[70] C.J.H. Wright, *Living as the People of God* p 180.

26

substitute for, the labour of free members of the household. In other words, slave labour was not a means by which free Israelites were released from physical labour, as was the case in classical Greece, for example.[71]

So, not only were slaves protected by the Torah in Israel, they also could expect to avoid the degradation of other slaves in history. In fact, it is precisely this attitude to slavery which makes Israel's law 'unquestionably unique in the ancient world'.[72] This Hebraic context should be borne in mind as we consider some of the relevant Pauline texts.

'If you can gain your freedom...' (1 Corinthians 7)

Paul here tackles one of several queries sent by the church, this time on marriage and singleness. In what initially seems to be a puzzling digression, he uses two apparently unrelated illustrations – one from contemporary ethnic divisions, the other from social status divisions. Unfortunately, the Greek of 7:21 contains some ambiguity. Dawes offers two alternative translations:

> does the sentence mean 'even supposing you could go free, you would be better off making the most of your slavery' (NAB) or 'although if you can gain your freedom, do so' (NIV)?[73]

Are the letter's recipients to understand 'slavery' as being better, or 'freedom'? Dawes concludes that the former is better (with the NIV), but his reasons are interesting. He shows how

---

[71] C.J.H. Wright, *Living as the People of God* p 178.
[72] C.J.H. Wright, *Living as the People of God* p 179.
[73] G.W. Dawes, *But if you can gain your freedom (1 Corinthians 7:17-24)* (Catholic Biblical Quarterly, Vol 52, 1990) p 689.

Paul's argument in the whole chapter demands this interpretation.

The apostle is treading a careful course between two extremes apparently prevalent in the Corinthian Church. Against the libertine elements in Corinth, Paul asserts that marriage is indissoluble (apart from the few circumstances outlined in vv 10-11 and v 15). Nevertheless, he insists that marriage is not always appropriate; singleness has benefits, an argument that has little to do with ascetics. Paul's position is summarised in 7:24 – 'in whatever condition you were called, brothers and sisters, there remain with God', presumably because one can be a godly, Spirit-filled Christian in either state.

It is while walking this tightrope that Paul uses the illustrations of circumcision and slavery. But why use two illustrations to make the same point? Closer examination shows that they are subtly different. The first illustration, that of circumcision, is startling in that it comes from Paul the ex-Pharisee. 'Circumcision is nothing, and uncircumcision is nothing.' (7:19) So circumcision is not what bars or guarantees inclusion into the people of God. Paul's central concern, then, is for disciples to remain in whatever circumstances they find themselves, whether circumcised or not, married or not.

Yet singleness still has advantages. Marriage might not impede one's potential for godliness, but theoretically, one can devote more time and energy to the Lord's work if one is unattached (7:32). Consequently, his second illustration proceeds to a slightly different point. Nowhere does he say 'freedom is nothing and slavery is nothing'. He is obviously not indifferent to these two, just as he is not indifferent about celibacy – he clearly has a preference for celibacy throughout the chapter. Hence:

[T]he slave who is offered the chance of becoming free ought to make use of this opportunity (v21b). In the same way (the implied argument goes), the person who is already celibate or who has been married and is now once again single is urged to take advantage of this opportunity to remain single-mindedly devoted to the Lord (cf. v 35).[74]

The context of the whole chapter points us towards the correct translation of v 21b. Paul has made clear that he is keen for people *not* to be enslaved. If they are enslaved, they should make the most of the opportunities to escape it (v 21). If they are free, then they should never allow themselves to become enslaved, for 'you were bought with a price' (v 23).[75] He does not seek revolution, nor does he endorse the institution.

'No longer as a slave ...' (Philemon)

Paul's letter to Philemon initially seems to contradict 1 Corinthians 7, because Paul actually sends Onesimus back to his 'rightful' owner, despite Onesimus's conversion (v 15-16):

> Perhaps this is the reason he was separated from you for a while, so that you might have him back forever, no longer as a slave but more than a slave, a beloved brother – especially to me but how much more to you, both in the flesh and in the Lord.

Perhaps Paul was simply responding to a specific pastoral situation, and this has little to contribute to the issue. However, it is possible to discern a consistent attitude behind what Paul did for both Philemon and Onesimus.

---

[74] Dawes, *But if you can gain your freedom* p 696.
[75] This intriguing verse could well allude to the temptation for Christians to sell themselves into slavery in order to avoid the insecurity and potential persecution that came inevitably with their open declarations of their faith.

Paul was in a difficult position, with a conflict between his convictions about obeying secular authorities (e.g. Romans 13), and his Torah-influenced attitudes to slavery. The former would have forced him to send a runaway straight back, whereas Deuteronomy 23:15-16 insisted on runaway slaves being given sanctuary. This is demonstrated by his two aims in writing the letter. Thus, Guthrie says:

> Paul's greatest anxiety does not seem to centre in the owner's willingness to allow Onesimus to stay with Paul, but the more serious consideration of whether he would be prepared to receive him at all. How else can [v17] be understood?[76]

This fulfilled his concern to comply with Roman law.

> At the same time there may well have been in Paul's mind the faint hope that the owner would go beyond his explicit request (cf. v21) and would release the slave for the work of the gospel.[77]

Paul would clearly have preferred Onesimus to be free and working.

So, in spite of appearances, *Philemon* is anything but a flat acquiescence to secular law. Paul certainly sent Onesimus back, but the vital point is that he sent him back as a Christian *brother*. Philemon could not miss the significance of this apostolic hint. This by itself had dramatic implications for slavery as a whole.

> What this letter does is to bring us into an atmosphere in which the institution could only wilt and die ... formal

---

[76] D. Guthrie, *New Testament Introduction*, 4th Edition (Leicester, Apollos, 1990) p 663.
[77] Guthrie, *New Testament Introduction* p 663.

emancipation would be but a matter of expediency, the technical confirmation of the new relationship that had already come into being.[78]

'Slaves, obey your earthly masters ...' (Colossians 3)

It is safe to conclude, then that Paul in *Philemon* was, at the very least, ambivalent towards slavery. This is entirely consistent with what he taught in 1 Corinthians 7. The problem comes in the household codes, where his views appear much less liberal. Nevertheless, even there, it is possible to detect a desire for change. Lincoln notes for example that there was 'striking reciprocity' between slaves and masters. Both were to determine their actions in terms of their relationship to Christ.[79] In Colossians at any rate, it is clear that a slave's eschatological status was secure, whatever his or her earthly circumstances, and this was to impact how masters treated them in this life.

So, we might summarise Paul's attitude to slavery in these terms. If a Christian was free, then under no circumstances should he or she go into slavery voluntarily. That would deny the very status that Christ had won for them on the cross. However, if a slave became a Christian, then because of their lack of autonomy, they had no choice but to accept the situation. The key principle was to live a godly life serving their master to the best of their abilities. Being a slave did not preclude a wholeheartedly Christian lifestyle. Yet if manumission was an option, it should be sought after, because freedom was clearly preferable.

---

[78] F.F. Bruce, *Paul – Apostle of the Free Spirit* (Exeter, Paternoster Press, 1977) p 401.
[79] Lincoln, *Ephesians* p 425.

Whatever one says about this summary, the fact is that Paul never endorsed slavery as an integral part of Christian service and holiness. It was never a status that should be maintained as permanent or a divinely ordained institution. In the very passage where Paul calls on people to remain in the state in which they were called (1 Corinthians 7), he encourages slaves to achieve manumission.

But what of the third relationship in the Galatians 3:28 proclamation? How does Paul treat women in the church? This is, of course, an area of great controversy, and a topic too vast to compass here. Consequently, the next discussion will have to be restricted to whether or not Paul's writing contains a consistent position on the role of women. We should then be able to assess more helpfully how Paul's teaching on slavery relates to Galatians 3:28.

(ii)   *The Attitude to Women in the Pauline Corpus*

It is striking that Paul argues for his position on the role of women from more than one foundation. Often, those arguing for a traditional position immediately go to 1 Timothy 2, which is a perplexing and highly debated text. There, a stringent subordinationist position seems to be related in some way to creation order and its relevance to a fallen world. However, this letter in itself is controversial as it is often held to be Deutero-Pauline and so is not considered a reliable source for Paul's thought.

Nevertheless, there is methodological consistency in the way Paul argues throughout the Pauline corpus. In his gloss on 'As is fitting in the Lord' (Colossians 3:18)[80], O'Brien discusses

---

[80] O'Brien, *Colossians & Philemon* p 222.

the scope of its implications. He points to the fact that there was a widely accepted recognition of some sort of created world order, supported by a passage in 1 Corinthians.

> Paul is not suggesting here that the woman is naturally or spiritually inferior to the man, or the wife to the husband. But he does mention elsewhere that there is a divinely instituted hierarchy in the order of creation, and in this order the wife follows that of her husband (1 Corinthians 11:3, 7-9. The hierarchical argument ... is made more explicit at Ephesians 5:23-24).[81]

There is a profound relationship between the first creation and the second, new creation. The Ephesians household code draws a precise link between the relationship of a husband to his wife (part of the first creation) and that of Christ to his church (the second). It is so profound, that it is often hard to see precisely which of these two relationships Paul is discussing in this section! He appears to meander between marriage and astounding ecclesiological statements. Consequently, we can easily forget that the context is a 'mundane' household code. Witherington notes that both the creational and ecclesiological foundations for headship can be found in Ephesians 5:

> Paul is well aware of the grounding that human marriage has in the story of Adam and Eve (v31a), but he is more concerned here to model Christian marriage on the pattern of the relationship of Christ and the Church. [82]

This startling link surely implies that Paul's understanding of headship falls beyond the bounds of common connotations of subordination. To his thinking, headship is profoundly reminiscent of the cross, because there he saw a model for its

---

[81] O'Brien, *Colossians & Philemon* p 222.
[82] Witherington, *Women in the Earliest Churches* p 55.

practice. The cross was how Christ expressed his love for the church, and that love is to shape the husband's responsibilities. As a result of this love, the church is expected to be prepared to submit to Christ; in the same but paradoxical way, the submission of the wife is a voluntary expression of her dignity. This can only be appreciated when it is seen in contrast to the prevailing views of women at Paul's time:

> Schrage and others claim that the basis, motivation and emphasis on the subordination of wives to husbands in the NT are different from similar injunctions elsewhere in the ancient world. The exhortation to be subordinate is balanced with the instruction to husbands to love their wives: the admonition is an appeal to free and responsible agents that can only be heeded voluntarily, never by the elimination or breaking of the human will, much less by means of a servile submissiveness; and finally its motivation is 'in the Lord'.[83]

Moreover, foundations for headship can be seen in an even more surprising location – the Trinity. Paul legitimates his teaching by appealing to the relationship between Christ and his bride, the church. But he may imply that the Trinity is a good ground for it as well. It is no accident that Paul avoids the word 'obey' when speaking of how wives should respond to their husbands, unlike both slaves and children. Instead, he uses the verb 'submit'. If the word's usage is traced throughout the New Testament, we find it applied in various contexts. In the middle or passive mood, it refers to all believers in relation to secular authority (Romans 13:1) or in relation to church officials (1 Peter 5:5) and even in relation to God and Christ (James 4:7, 1 Peter 5:6). However, more pertinently to this discussion, Paul applies it to Christ in relation to the Father:

---

[83] O'Brien, *Colossians & Philemon* p 222.

> When all things are subjected to him, then the Son himself
> will also be subjected to the one who put all things in
> subjection under him, so that God may be all in all. (I
> Corinthians 15:28)

Crucially, Witherington demonstrates the significance of this:

> That the verb is used of Christ likely indicates that it does
> not indirectly imply an idea of inferiority of the submitter to
> the one submitted to, so far as their personhood or worth is
> concerned. Rather it appears to have more to do with
> following the example of Christ who willingly humbled
> himself to the Father.[84]

Christ was not inferior to the Father. His status and identity as
fully human and fully divine are axiomatic to the faith.
However, his role is different from that of the Father, and it is
this in part which differentiates the two persons (though care is
needed here, lest one descend into Modalism). Nowhere is this
paradox more explicit in the New Testament than in John's
gospel.

This insight demonstrates the consistency in Paul's
thought. He ascribes astonishing degrees of mutuality to the
male-female relationship. For example in I Corinthians 7 he is
determined to apply his teaching equally to men and women,
husbands and wives. Almost every injunction has its
symmetrical counterpart to the opposite sex. Nowhere is this
more evident than at the start of the chapter (vv 3-4), in his
directions about sexual relations for married couples.

Witherington argues that what Paul is doing in
Ephesians 5 is trying to destroy the contemporary subjugation
of women by men, by putting the relationship in a divine

---

[84] Witherington, *Women in the Earliest Churches* p 50; cf. O'Brien,
Colossians & Philemon p 221.

perspective. This equally applies to 1 Corinthians 7. It is a question of reform, rather than removal:

> This is Paul's deliberate attempt to reform the patriarchal structure of his day, a structure he inherited, adopted, and adapted. Paradoxically, however, the effect was also to ground that revised patriarchal structure involving the husband's headship in the eternal relationship between Christ and Church. This serves to give an ongoing and permanent theological rationale for the husband's headship and wife's submission.[85]

Mutuality for men and women is preserved, as is the status of being equal children of Christ, and all of this within a subordinationist framework. The important thing is to understand this framework as Paul understands it, not as our contemporary culture does (which often makes it out to be intrinsically and necessarily oppressive). Thus it is impossible to categorise the apostle as either a chauvinist or feminist.[86]

There is no escaping headship in Paul. But it is couched in very different terms to the relationship between slaves and masters. There is no   equivalent: he never called on women to escape from their male 'oppressors' if they could. This was because the marriage bond had deep theological significance and because he did not see the husband-wife relationship in a negative light. This is not to say that he viewed his contemporary patriarchal society in glowing terms – far from it. There was much to change, as has already been argued throughout this chapter.

Whereas slavery was an institution that threatened the Christian's freedom and status in Christ and was thus to be

---

[85] Witherington, *Women in the Earliest Churches* p 55.
[86] cf. Witherington, *Women in the Earliest Churches* p 41.

avoided, headship never had this connotation for Paul. It was grounded on the eternal work and purposes of Christ and therefore was to model itself upon his relationships, both to the church and the Father. As Witherington says, this gives it 'an ongoing and permanent theological rationale'. Paul's declaration in Galatians 3:28 never subverted the principle of headship. This explains the proximity of the Colossians equivalent (3:11) to the household code. Even though male/female equality is not explicitly mentioned in Colossians 3:11, the similarity to Galatians leads to the conclusion that this was not far from Paul's mind. If Paul knew what he was doing in writing the letter, and is consistent within it, then this distinction between role and status is the only satisfying explanation of what Paul means.

(iii)   A Brief Point about Children

If there are no distinctions within the household codes, what happens to the relationship between children and parents? Is this to be cast out as yet another relationship that Paul sought to reform with a view to its ultimate demise? Is this an inherently oppressive relationship? Of course, there are people in today's society who regard it in this way, especially in the face of widespread sexual abuse by family members. It has even been suggested that future directives on Children's Rights from the European Union could be interpreted as implying that the family is oppressive.[87]

However, there are few Christians who would be prepared to go this far. Therefore they are forced into either inconsistency or an acceptance of the principle of distinctions

---

[87] I am grateful to Jock MacGregor of the L'Abri Fellowship for this point.

within the household codes. Thus, Knight notes:

> [T]he demise of slavery does not sweep this permanent moral command for children away; for the two relationships are not inseparably connected as to their essence, but only exist side-by-side because slavery fit into the larger household setting of the day.[88]

3.4. Conclusion

We have seen that Paul did indeed assume a distinction between the different members of the household addressed in his household codes. Of course, there are similarities, but he clearly considered the roles of husbands/wives and fathers/children to be binding, despite his Galatians 3:28 declaration. The same cannot be said for slavery.

> Thus there is a great divide between husbands and wives, and parents and children on one side of this list of household relationships, and masters and slaves on the other side.[89]

In order to make sense of this apparent contradiction, one must remember the distinction between status and role, a distinction which our contemporary society finds hard to appreciate.[90]

---

[88] G. Knight, "Husbands and Wives as Analogues of Christ and the Church" in Piper & Grudem (ed), *Recovering Biblical Manhood and Womanhood* (Wheaton, Crossway, 1991) p 176.

[89] Knight, "Husbands and Wives as Analogues of Christ and the Church" p 177.

[90] This is because too often a person's status in society is confused with their role. Their status is all too often actually derived from their role. The Christian is very different – their status comes from being a child of God and co-heir with Christ, and their role is immaterial here. (Hence, 1 Corinthians 7:21-24, and Romans 8:17: 'and if children, then heirs, heirs of God and joint heirs with Christ – if, in fact, we suffer with him so that we may also be

Therefore, the anti-abolitionists were wrong to bind the slavery issue so closely with a threat to Paul's teaching on the role of women. One can see within the epistles a clear differentiation between the two.

4. Final Thoughts

The presence of slavery in the New Testament causes some contemporary readers considerable anxiety, especially if they hold to a more traditional view of scriptural authority. No one today could conceivably wish to reinstate the institution and we rightly rejoice in the achievements of the eighteenth and nineteenth century Abolitionists. The resurgence of interest in their achievements has renewed the need for clarity about precisely what ethical precedents they established. This is in large part because of the prevalence of the 'trajectory' argument. Often on the basis of Galatians 3:28 and other passages, interpreters have discerned a desire on Paul's part to see liberation won for others as well as for slaves. Thus the abolition of slavery is commonly seen as a precedent for the emancipation of women and their roles in church life, and now is even applied to homosexuality. This paper has not sought to discuss either of those contentious issues in depth but has been confined to what the New Testament teaches about slavery and how that impacts the women's debate in particular.

We have approached the subject from a number of different angles, all the time seeking to understand the historical context and connotations of New Testament slavery. We have seen that there were substantial differences between

---

glorified with him.')

Roman slavery and the institution we readily associate it with, namely American slavery. The ancient system was much more fluid and ambiguous than its more modern counterpart, and certainly had little to do with race. Paul was not entirely accepting of the *status quo* in his day as careful exegesis of the relevant texts has shown. His concern was certainly reform and it is fair to say that if confronted with Deep South slavery, he would probably have been far more stringent.

Examining the texts (in particular the household codes of Ephesians and Colossians) has also provided the opportunity to assess the inter-relationship of slavery with the role of women. The two issues are clearly bound together in some way in Paul's household codes and the famous Galatians 3:28 reference. However, while there may well be good reasons for thinking that the traditional view of the role of women should be overthrown, it is the contention of this paper that this is not possible on the basis of a trajectory within the household codes. The differences between the role of slaves and women in the Christian household are too significant for a simplistic, blanket approach for each group. After all, few would suggest today that what applies to slaves and masters automatically applies to children and parents. The purpose here has been simply to plead for a rigour that does not rely on an unthinking use of the abolition of slavery as a precedent for abolishing biblical norms, whether they be in the realm of marriage relationships or wider sexual ethics. Slavery, whatever the parallels with other issues, is not a legitimate tool in the argument. Its abolition was certainly a great victory to be rejoiced in but was not the precedent it is often held to be.